Disney Princess Celebrations

Disney PRINCESS

CELEBRATE with Cinderella

Plan a Royal Party

Niki Ahrens

Lerner Publications ◆ Minneapolis

For Becky

Lerner Publications Company
An imprint of Lerner Publishing Group, Inc.
241 First Avenue North
Minneapolis, MN 55401 USA

For reading levels and more information, look up this title at www.lernerbooks.com.

Main body text set in Billy Infant.
Typeface provided by Sparky Type.

Library of Congress Cataloging-in-Publication Data

Names: Ahrens, Niki, 1979- author.
Title: Celebrate with Cinderella : plan a royal party / Niki Ahrens.
Description: Minneapolis : Lerner Publications, [2020] | Series: Disney
    princess celebrations | Includes bibliographical references and index.
Identifiers: LCCN 2019011664 (print) | LCCN 2019012996 (ebook) |
    ISBN 9781541582767 (eb pdf) | ISBN 9781541572744 (lib. bdg.)
Subjects: LCSH: Handicraft—Juvenile literature.
Classification: LCC TT160 (ebook) | LCC TT160 .A3323 2020 (print) |
    DDC 745.5—dc23

LC record available at https://lccn.loc.gov/2019011664

Manufactured in the United States of America
1-46541-47586-7/16/2019

Table of Contents

A Royal Party

How do you show kindness? Cinderella cares for the people and animals around her. Show you care for others when you host a royal party! You'll need to do these things:

- Get the permission of a parent or guardian to host a party. Send invitations to your guests.

- Create your decorations, party favors, and treats.

- Tidy the party space!

- Show courage by leading royal activities.

- Clean up after the party, and send thank-you notes to your guests for attending.

Host with Heart

- 🎃 Invite someone you don't know well, and make a new friend.

- 🎃 Care for your guests by being aware of food allergies.

- 🎃 Create party crafts on top of newspaper to avoid making a mess.

- 🎃 Be safe in the kitchen, and wash your hands before making any treats.

- 🎃 Start and end on time to make sure the magic doesn't fade away!

- 🎃 Kindly include every guest.

- 🎃 Recycle all materials that you can afterward.

- 🎃 Work hard so everyone has a ball!

Royal Seal Invitations

Invitations to Prince Charming's royal ball were stamped with a royal seal. Add your special seal to your invitations.

Materials

- cork

- craft glue

- 3-inch (7.6 cm) piece of string

- scissors

- 8½-by-11-inch (22 by 28 cm) sheets of paper

- marker

- ink pad

- 4½-by-9½-inch (11 by 24 cm) envelopes

1. Stand the cork on one flat end. Coat the other end with glue.

2. Place the piece of string on the glued end of the cork. Shape the string into a special design. Cut any extra string off your design. Set the cork aside until the glue is completely dry.

3. Write your invitation on paper. Include the party date, time, and location.

Party Tip! Did You Know?

A seal is a symbol used to show who sent a document. Seals are commonly made by stamping pictures into soft wax. A royal seal proves that a document is from a monarchy.

4. Stamp the string design on the ink pad. Then stamp your special seal on the invitation.

5. Fold your invitation into thirds, and tuck it in an envelope.

6. Stamp your seal across the envelope's seal. Send each guest an invitation.

You are invited to a royal party! I hope you can join.

Date _____
Time _____
Place _____
RSVP _____

Pumpkin Carriage Decorations

Cinderella rides to the ball in an elegant coach. Her fairy godmother transformed it from a pumpkin! Decorate your party with 3-D carriages.

Materials

- orange or blue construction paper

- scissors

- hole punch

- yellow and white pipe cleaners

- pencil

- clear tape

1. Fold the sheet of paper in half, matching the shorter sides. Then fold it in half twice more in the same direction.

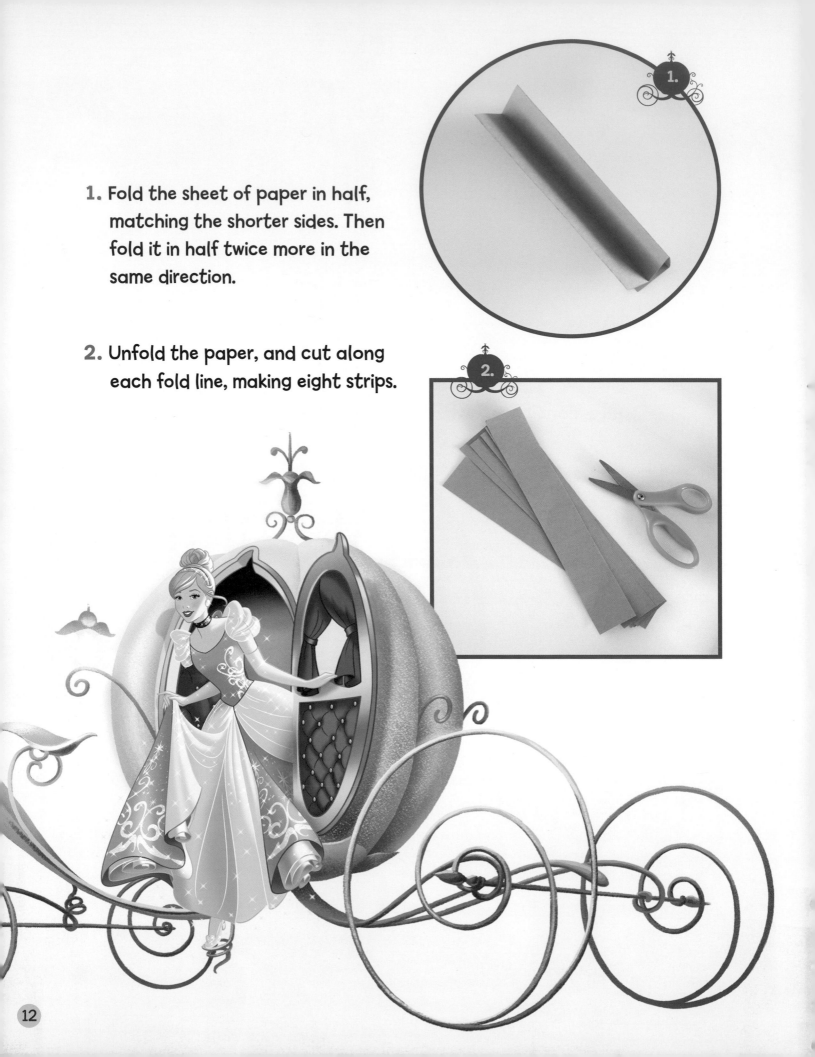

2. Unfold the paper, and cut along each fold line, making eight strips.

3. Stack the eight strips on top of one another. Punch a hole at each end of the stack. Thread a pipe cleaner's ends through the holes.

4. Slide both stacked ends toward the pipe cleaner's center to form a paper arch.

5. Carefully separate the stacked strips into a sphere.

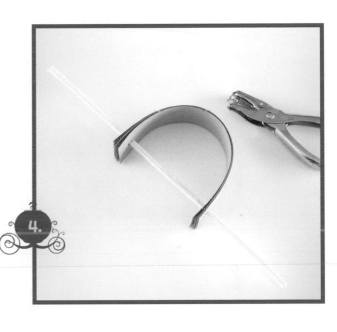

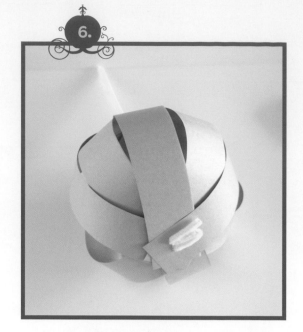

6. Fold one end of the pipe cleaner flat against the bottom of the sphere.

7. Wrap the rest of the pipe cleaner around a pencil to make a curly pumpkin stem design.

8. Bend four pipe cleaners into loose spirals to make wheels. Tape the outer end of each wheel behind a paper strip.

Magic Wand Treats

The Fairy Godmother casts spells with her wand to get Cinderella ready for the ball. Serve fruit wands for a magical treat.

Materials

- cutting board

- small cookie cutter

- wooden skewers

Ingredients

This recipe makes 6 to 8 servings.

- 2 cups grapes or berries

- 5 to 6 watermelon slices

- 1 cup cantaloupe or pineapple chunks

1. Wash your hands and rinse the grapes or berries.

2. Place a watermelon slice on the cutting board. Use the cookie cutter to cut out shapes from a watermelon slice. Set this aside.

3. Carefully slide about five pieces of fruit onto a skewer, starting at its pointed end and pushing each piece down the stick to make room for the next piece. Leave room at the base of the skewer for holding.

4. Gently slide the watermelon shape onto the top of the wand.

5. Assemble more fruit wands to make delicious, magical treats!

Party Tip! Be Earth-Friendly
You may have extra fruit left over after assembling the wands. Put the extra pieces in a bowl to make a fruit salad.

Dance in Glass Slippers

When Cinderella's glass slipper fits, the Prince's search ends. Create sparkling slippers that fit just right for everyone.

Materials

- metallic cardstock

- pencil

- scissors

- hole punch

- glue stick

- foil pieces, sequins, or craft jewels

- 24-inch (61 cm) ribbon

1. Set your foot on the cardstock. Trace all the way around your foot with a pencil.

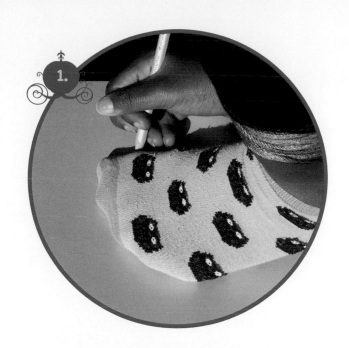

2. Draw a shoe's heel at the back of your tracing on the same side of the outline as your pinky toe.

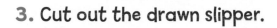

3. Cut out the drawn slipper.

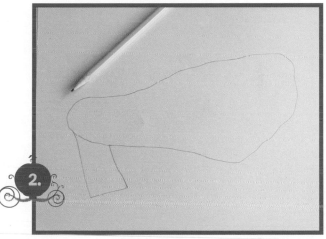

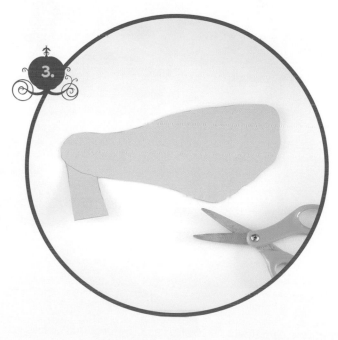

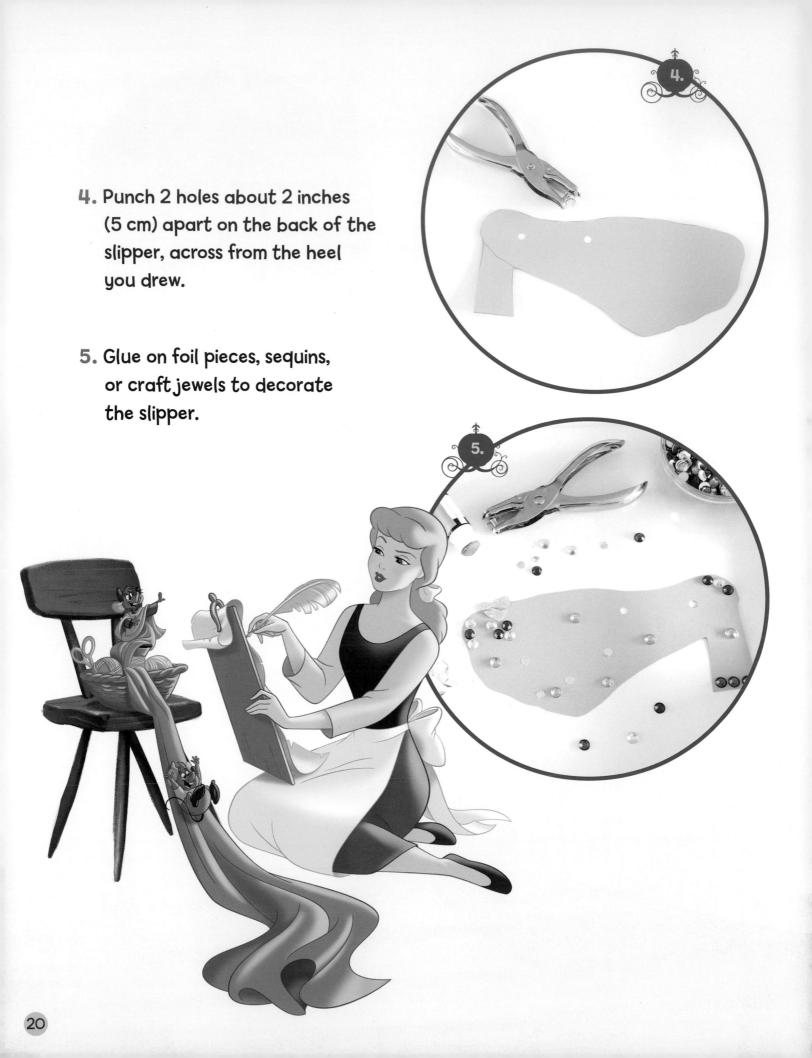

4. Punch 2 holes about 2 inches (5 cm) apart on the back of the slipper, across from the heel you drew.

5. Glue on foil pieces, sequins, or craft jewels to decorate the slipper.

6. Thread a ribbon through the 2 punched holes. Loosely tie your slipper around your ankle.

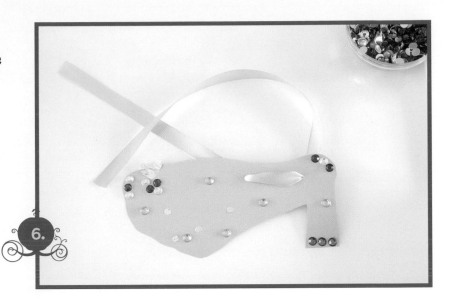

6.

Party Tip! Be Respectful

Show your kindness for others by letting your friends go first in choosing their craft materials. Praise all your guests for their beautiful slipper creations.

Birdfeeder Party Favors

Cinderella's sweet songbird friends help brighten her days. Upcycle cardboard tubes into birdfeeders that your guests can lovingly share with feathered friends.

Materials

- hole punch

- cardboard tube

- nut or sun butter

- rubber scraper

- large bowl of wild birdseed

- 3-foot (0.9 m) piece of string

- craft stick

- craft glue

1. Use a hole punch to make two holes across from each other on one end of the cardboard tube.

2. Spread a layer of nut or sun butter around the outside of the tube with a rubber scraper.

3. Roll the buttered tube in a bowl of birdseed to cover it.

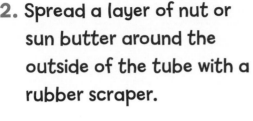

4. Thread a string through the birdfeeder's holes and tie the ends in a knot.

5. Glue a stick perch across the tube's bottom. Allow the glue to dry.

6. Make a birdfeeder to send home with each guest!

Party Tip! Did You Know?
Bluebirds have had important meanings in many different cultures throughout history. They have been symbols of sun, hope, and happiness.

Thank-You Mice

Cinderella's mouse friends Jaq and Gus help her with chores. Send heartfelt mouse notes to thank your guests.

Materials

- 8½-by-11-inch (22 by 28 cm) sheets of construction paper

- pencil

- scissors

- pen

- small cup

- pink paper

- craft glue

- googly eyes

- buttons

- clear tape

- several 4-inch (10 cm) pieces of string

1. Fold a sheet of construction paper in half, matching the shorter sides. From the fold line, draw a large half heart.

2. Cut out this half heart from both layers.

3. Unfold the heart. Write a kind and thankful message inside.

4. Fold the heart again, and turn it so the fold line is at the bottom. This will be the bottom of the mouse's body.

Dear

Thank you from the bottom of my heart for making the party dreamy! ♡

Sincerely,

5. Set a small cup upside down on the pink paper. Trace around it, and then cut the circle out to make an ear.

6. Glue the ear, a googly eye, and a button nose to your mouse.

7. Tape a string tail on the back of the mouse.

8. Send a thank-you mouse to every guest!

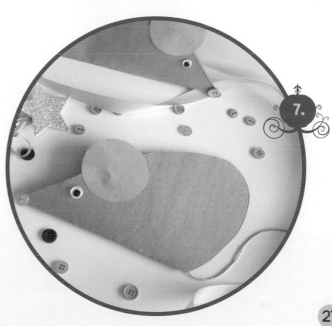

Dream Your Party

Cinderella shows generosity to her friends and never gives up in hard situations. Being brave in a new situation helps her follow her dreams. What wishes do you have for your party? Imagine ways you could celebrate kindness with your guests. Dreaming up party activities is half the fun. Have a royal ball planning your celebration!

Glossary

courage: a feeling of bravery

generosity: being kind and willing to give help or support

guest: a person who attends an event or party

host: to hold an event or party

monarchy: power and rule by one person, such as a queen or king

royal: related to the queen, king, or their family

seal: a stamp or mark that shows who sent a document

upcycle: to reuse something for arts and crafts instead of throwing it away

To Learn More

BOOKS

Ahrens, Niki. *Celebrate with Moana: Plan a Wayfinding Party.*
Minneapolis: Lerner Publications, 2020.
Moana fans will love learning how to plan the perfect wayfinding party!

Boothroyd, Jennifer. *Disney Princess Top 10s: From Ariel to Rapunzel*
Minneapolis: Lerner Publications, 2019.
Look back at funny, inspiring, and determined moments for Disney princesses.

WEBSITES

Cinderella: Never Give Up
https://princess.disney.com/cinderella
Take fun quizzes, play games, and learn all about Cinderella.

Every Cinderella Reference in the New Cinderella
https://ohmy.disney.com/movies/2015/09/15/every-cinderella
-reference-in-the-new-cinderella/
Enjoy and compare two versions of this magical story.

Have a Ball with These Memorable Cinderella Quotes
https://ohmy.disney.com/news/2018/05/08/cinderella-quotes/
Revisit your favorite *Cinderella* characters' best lines.

Index

PHOTO CREDITS

Additional photos: art_of_sun/Shutterstock.com, p. 2;
Julia Sudnitskaya/Shutterstock.com, p. 3; 5 second Studio/
Shutterstock.com, p. 5T; Rawpixel.com/Shutterstock.com,
p. 5B; Matt Benoit/Shutterstock.com, p. 7. Cover and
design elements: Susii/Shutterstock.com (balloons);
YamabikaY/Shutterstock.com (glitter); surachet khamsuk/
Shutterstock.com (glitter).